Where Flora Sings

First published 2020 by The Hedgehog Poetry Press

Published in the UK by
The Hedgehog Poetry Press
5, Coppack House
Churchill Avenue
Clevedon
BS21 6QW

www.hedgehogpress.co.uk

ISBN: 978-1-913499-43-3

9 8 7 6 5 4 3 2 1

A CIP Catalogue record for this book is available from the
British Library.

Printed by TJ Books Limited

Where Flora Sings

by

Margaret Royall

In Memoriam

Where Flora Sings is dedicated to
Virginia Mustard (my dear late friend Ginnie)
who loved all flowers, especially sunflowers

Contents

Section 1

Flower Power / People Power

BUTTERCUP

'Tilt your chin,' she said,
deftly plucking a buttercup
from among the daisies –
'Let's see if you like butter!'

I obey as she holds the
flower head beneath my jaw,
sensing a radiant golden warmth
tingling on my three-year-old chin.

'Oh yes you do,'she laughs,
a tinkling laugh of motherhood,
the kind of laugh you remember
long after death has snatched her away.

MARIGOLD

That's how he remembered
the way to pronounce her name -
She hated him calling her Mahri
or M'rie. No, it was Marry,
as in Marigold.

He stared at the flower beds
aching with burnt orange blooms,
a shower of innocent petals
dispersing on the gusting wind.
How rude that on first meeting
he'd called her Carrot Top!
Her mane of Titian-red curls
had been his undoing;
That flowing Rossetti-esque hair
unleashed a cloying madness in him.
He fell for her wildness,
refused to look at anyone else.

But like the flowers her
affections blew with the wind.
She plucked those innocent petals,
scattered them carelessly where
fields were greener, broke his heart
with her Marry-gold curse.

DAISY CHAINS

'Let me show you how to
weave a daisy chain.
Pierce a hole in the stem,
thread another one through,
make a garland fit for a princess,'
that's what my granny used to say.

Adorned with daisy-chains
woven around our young limbs
we danced together through
wildflower meadows, wearing our
dresses with matching knickers -
'All Things Bright and Beautiful'
dresses, that's what we called them.
We clutched our threadbare teddies,
naive Lolita clones that we were then,
playing in the sunshine, seizing the day,
following the instinctive code of
'Carpe Diem,' blissfully unaware
of life's inherent dangers.

WILD POPPIES

These poppies have not
grown wild on fields of battle,
they grew in my heart;
small seeds of grace born from love,
sown more in hope than in grief.

The rain has watered
their roots deep set in the clay,
sung them lullabies
at dusk and in the half-light
of dawn has kissed them awake.

Each one a dear friend,
remembered fondly every
day, held close in prayer,
like blood-red droplets trickling
from a wound which never heals.

PASQUE FLOWER MARY MAGDALENE

Tight buds of purple-blue encircled
by ferns of fine filigree, unfolding
gracious petals in Easter flowering;
a pure pascal offering.

Hair silky soft akin to Mary Magdalene,
exuding modest simplicity, just like her;
a truly uplifting sight. With the call
of spring in their sap,

they turn nodding faces to the sun,
reflecting biblical prophecies fulfilled.
Sown in the dark days of winter,
they push through the hard soil,

emerging from their Gethsemane tomb,
cocooned in robes befitting a king.
Their name invokes the joy
of that first Easter Day.

As Mary witnessed in disbelief the empty tomb,
so too this shy pasque flower bears witness
to the miracle of resurrection, emerging
each spring from harsh midwinter chill.

INVOCATION TO SPRING

Come now, sweet Spring!
Mow me down a meadow of clover,
Fill me a wheelbarrow of hay
and water the earth with raindrops.
Sing me a tree full of birds,
Dance me a stream of milk white clouds,
Warm me a bed beneath the cherry blossom
and fill my heart with sheer delight.

Come now, sweet Spring!
Light me a Beltane fire on the first of May,
Chase me to the fresh-blown woods
and tempt me to lie with you by the brook.
Paint me visions of sunshine and rainbows
Weave me a carpet of bluebells,
Send me the Green Man for company
and fill my soul with the bounty of May.

CROCOSMIA

They bloom in gardens by the Sound,
dancing in the late summer sun
among rocks of lewisian gneiss;

sentinels along the rugged paths
through ruined Nunnery grounds
down to the sandy shore...

blazing stems of orange, yellow,
fiery coral-red pokers
bursting from tiny pods,

like minute pebbles
forming endless ripples
on stone-skimmed ponds.

Turning modest heads
they willingly perform
for my delight,

as I pause by the garden gate,
leaning in to inhale
the early morning scents and sounds.

They are the last image in my head
before sleep and the first flash
of morning inspiration....

Their familiar greeting
tells me this is where
I am meant to be.

SUMMER MEADOWS

Cooperation is the buzzword;
harmonious consensus.
Opulent symphonies with
Nature the sentient conductor.
Poppy, ranunculus and kingcup
rising and falling in gentle cadence
with cornflower, salvia and forget-me-not;
a fragrant patchwork in the sweet grass,
like an eco rainbow, tipping the earth,
radiant with inner beauty.
A ballet of delicate blooms
dressed in powder-puff tutus,
thoughtfully choreographed,
dancing to the tune of sun, wind and rain.

Wildflower meadows echo the vibe
of cottage gardens in a bygone age....
Green spaces flourishing
with aphids, beetles, butterflies,
moths and caterpillars,
bumble bee numbers multiplied tenfold -
that gentle, hypnotic hum reassuring
as they delve in the throats of foxgloves.
The project enhances both water and soil,
a winning outcome for biota.
This wild beauty brings closer
the goal of a greener future.
Just stop and look!
Paradise stretches out
before your eyes,
a triumph of rewilding.

BULBS AWAIT THE CALL OF SPRING

So still they lie, snuggled up, clinging to life
through the dark, chill winter days,
tucked up where icy finger tips cannot pry,
warm in their safe cocoon below earth,
oblivious to Jack Frost's chilly breath
swirling above their musty leaf-mould bed.
Trees moan as snow weighs down boughs
and rotten branches are severed.

So still they lie, curled in a foetal ball
of comfort, winter-proof hibernation.
The worms may grub around them,
eager to lick salt from their brittle roots,
yet they dream on cosily in the luxury
of oblivion, a strange limbo, held for a
season in a magical fairy world, until the
weak warmth of February kisses them awake.

SISSINGHURST AT MIDSUMMER

A veil lifts between earth and sky,
revealing a lush green paradise,
its mullioned windows thrown open
to the gardens....

Mood music captivates:
Harp song through tall grass,
bees crooning in lupin throats,
swallows darting overhead.
The ambiance is relaxing;
sight, smell and sound seamlessly
fused together in a heady symphony.
Bouquet of rose, lavender and herbs
tease the sharpening senses.
Crooked chimneys peer down onto
exquisite garden-rooms full-bloomed
with a riot of colour.

Oast houses nestle in the shade
of the castle tower.
Along paved walks bemused statues
observe the constant parade of visitors,
all curious to experience this romantic
idyll created by Vita and Harold*....
An enchanted corner of Kent, wrapping
visitors in a cloak of midsummer magic.

*Vita Sackville West and Harold Nicholson, creators of Sissinghurst gardens

A WOODLAND WEDDING

Today I chanced upon a bride and groom
Together with their friends in woodland glade,
All dressed in velvet cloaks with rosebud crowns,
Huge altar stones around the coppice laid.
It was a pretty sight, fasting of hands,
Proclaiming their sweet love and dancing round.
The woodland nymphs triumphant joined the throng
While hares and rabbits watched from lower ground.
For rings they'd woven rushes from the stream
and prettied them with daisies yellow and white.
Around their necks hung scented wreaths of lilac -
These fairy folk made such a glorious sight.
Titania and Oberon came too,
And fairy music played the whole night through.

A SPRING TRILOGY

(i)

The Vernal equinox
brings a metamorphosis,
a gradual unseen flowering,
winter still in its last gasp
as the magic unfurls.
Galanthi drift like snowflakes,
virgin white for first communion,
silently waiting for Lent bells' chime.
In their innocence they cling
to lush green stems, devout heads
nodding in the gusting breeze,
humming messages from snow gods

(ii)

Zephyros weaves his April magic,
bringing a rush to the beck,
thrumming over sharp stones
in the rough-hewn stream bed.
The surge mounts, slapping against
the arches of the drovers' bridge,
carrying broken twigs downstream.
Overhead a swarm of mayfly nymphs,
hatched under safety of twilight,
hover above the water
like a great smoky breath...
Nature breathes a sigh of relief
after a lengthy drought, poised
for spring's first flowering
of apple and cherry blossom.

(iii)

A shiver of old-English bluebells
catches the eye.
In a hidden corner of the yard
they nestle apologetically
beneath the bay hedge,
breath held in anticipation
of the swallows' return.
In robes of royal blue-purple
they hint at the pomp and passion
soon to explode upon the scene.
Presently the cuckoo will contest
nesting rights with pipits and warblers
while the Witch men, sensing
the lure of Beltane in their bones,
will once more clash sticks on village greens.
The Spring pageant is set for renewal.

AMARYLLIS

Such beauty takes my breath away!
Sitting there, tall and proud,
inviting adoration.
At first glance flamingo pink,
yet no, too quick a judgement!
This amaryllis flower is multi-layered,
Closer inspection tells a greater truth,
its strands of colour blended seamlessly together.

At birth displaying gentle tangerine
with inner bell of warmest apricot pink,
it toiled majestically upwards towards
the weak light of first Spring....
Much bolder then the shades became,
blood red tendrils interspersed
with splashes of coral and ruby red.

Now all too soon the glory starts to fade
and withering petals glow defiant crimson,
as though they're holding back a loss of blood
and clinging to the last vestiges of life.
This sweet enchantment fills the morning space,
warms up the chilly air of early March.
Sweet memories of this colourful profusion
will stay forever locked within my heart.

WITHERED SUNFLOWERS

Les Tournesols Flétris

Turning he caught sight of her in the sunflower field,
Opening her arms wide, inviting him to join her.
Unperturbed by the scorching midday sun, she
Reached out to grasp his hand like a drowning child.
Not for a moment did he doubt the sincerity of her smile,
Eagerly vaulting the gate, trampling the flowers to reach her.
Suddenly she was gone, disappearing into the burnished gold.
Oh how he searched, leaving flowers there for her every day...
Love unrequited, the golden promise withered and died.

A VINTAGE ROSE

Her face is yesterday's rose......beautifully crumpled,
mapping out ancient well-trodden byways,
shedding fragrant petals to reveal an inner luminescence,
a scent of musk permeating the patchwork beauty.

Flashbacks dart across the mind's eye like butterflies:
ritual bathing at the healing well, drinking chalice water,
dancing on dewdrop toes beneath rippling willows,
weaving garlands in the dark silence of druids' caves.

A voluptuousness, trickling from a love spoon,
her once youthful skin deliciously etched by the sands of time,
still radiating that irresistible lure of vintage charisma -
the face of an English Rose, reborn in its third age.

RHODODENDRON TRIUMPH

Written in the grounds of Rydal Hall, Cumbria

They move with grace, these fuchsia-robed flamenco dancers,
Skirts ruffled and frilled, performing ad hoc *escobillas* –

You can almost hear the sharp click of the castanets!
Layer upon layer, overhanging the tree stumps by the rustic fence,

A merry-go-round of whirling dervishes in the fresh-blown flora,
Ablaze with glory, arrogant in their very magnificence.

So startling are they that passers-by stop in their tracks,
Lingering in awe to drink in this May extravaganza.

They dominate the garden, overshadowing the timid bluebells
Basking below, humbly resigned to a more lowly place.

A family of Herdwick sheep, out for their constitutional
Stop on the path to witness the performance overhead,

Subtly accompanied by Neptune's resident orchestra,
As cascades from the Force nearby gather momentum.

The music rises to a crescendo as the flamenco dance peaks -
But only the *aficionados* may observe this tender triumph

THE HOLLY AND THE IVY

When halls were decked with holly and ivy
In midwinter chill, when hope faded fast,
The Druids knew well they created a promise
that spring's lush green mantle would always grow back.
Whatever the weather they combed the near woods
for evergreen branches and berries blood red
to fashion their solstice wreaths, tying them fast
around hearths and in kitchens, above marriage beds:
Bold symbols of wedded love, friendship, fertility,
speaking to man of his sure immortality....
Revelling like Bacchus, like Saturn great feasting,
respite from dreariness, white candles glowing
to light up the blessings of nature's abundance,
good health for the sick and prosperity unceasing

These rites still prevail in the fabric of earth
And we still gather berries and deck out our homes,
Using these symbols to mark Christian birth,
Forgetting their origin on old pagan stones.

A FRENCH POTAGER IN JULY

The heat is stifling.
Storms hang in the air;
no respite from the sun
soaring high above,
withering flora and fauna.

Lazy is the buzzword today...
Dogs snooze in the potager,
rubbing itchy backs
against cool stone walls
overhung with wisteria.

A mother pigeon perches
on a precarious nest
beneath crumbling eaves,
flapping her wings
to cool her fledgling young.

Lovers prostrate on daybeds,
limbs entwined,
feed on the cool breath
from the whirring fan....
too hot to make love.

Yet no one should complain!
The icy blasts of winter
will arrive all too soon,
and memories of sultry
August heat will fade,
along with the dying wisteria..

A DEMENTIA SUFFERER ATTEMPTS REWILDING

Fingers gnarled by time's relentless curse
tremble as she rips the seed packet open

Mary, Mary, pick up your willow basket,
it's time to make your garden grow again!

Seeds rattle, jangle like forest creatures'
sudden chatter, fierce raindrops after drought

Mary, will you sow sweet meadow flowers
in wild profusion as you did as a child?

Seeds spill out, jewels sacrificed from April's crown;
a chain of broken gems cascading, scattering

Time waits for no man, Mary, be quick now,
Swoop like a magpie, make your garden grow!

They hit the cobbles, roll into far flung crevices
The eager soil receives no sustenance

Oh Mary, nothing good will come of this!
They say that you are too contrary, girl

On scissor hands and groaning knees she grubs around,
gathering up her grains of cruel dementia

How will your garden thrive now, Mary?
Nature alone cannot turn weeds to flowers!

A frisson of guilt travels down her crumpling spine
Somehow she must rewild this cottage plot

Oh Mary, Mary, soon it will be too late,
Call up your pretty maids to plant and sow!

She wrings her hands, fumbles with her apron strings,
slumps against the door jamb, all hope spent.

LADY WITH LAVENDER AURA

From a secret drawer Aunt Phoebe
takes the unctuous lavender oil - and

gaggles of barefoot children run amok through
wildflower meadows, dry tongues of summer

yearning for sarsaparilla and calamine balm
to soothe the itch of post-war deprivation.

She hears the electric hum of bees in lupin throats,
watches fingers pluck flowers from air-raid shelter walls,

Breathes in carbolic soap from the hard-scrubbed nails
of her dad, stripped off to wash in the kitchen sink,

Drools as her mum lifts milk-topped scones from
the blackened side-oven - Mrs Beaton's, of course.

On elbow crooks and freckled wrists she drips
the oil, cuts on her fingers stinging like vinegar.

Too much, intoxicating, filling her pretty head
with sickly-sweet confusion – gasping for breath,

wheezing from the burn of excess, as though
the lavender fields might soon be pulped to dust –

Those fields in France, crackling with spit-roast
hedgehogs, where carefree gypsies danced, caroused

and jumped the devil's cinders, their nostrils teased
by a lavender sea, infused with basil and thyme.

An idyll in a bottle, nostalgia's pangs released
whenever Aunt Phoebe performs her daily toilette.

Her clockwork days marked out in rhythmic bursts
Obedient daughter to family expectations

FASHIONISTA FIONA

Tall and talkative,
wittily entertaining,
yet a sensitive soul,
that's Fi!

In the grey months of waterlogged
fields and blustering gales,
when townies huddle in
coffee shops for warmth,
she brings a touch of light relief with her
tie-dye forget-me-not shawls,
her Indian silk skirts fringed with tulips,
Moroccan leather slippers laced with
myrtle leaves, all worn with great
panache, of course.
Her elegant Philip Treacy hats turn heads
as she sashays through the shopping mall.
Self-styled ambassador of fashion
she inspires all who watch her pass by
to dress in their vintage flower-power best.

VIEW FROM A COTTAGE WINDOW IN MARCH

raging beast of March
sweeps across the trembling earth
trees bend low in awe

newborn lambs run free
hillsides white with cotton wool
shepherds' hands need skill

tulip bulbs push through
jonquil bells chime on the air
storm-defying chords

fragile nests teeter
hedge, tree and house eaves bursting
predators find prey

daylight usurps night
hearts and minds attune to Spring
creation fulfilled

FLOWERS FOR A GHOST

Teatime now and still no one there...
She checks the date on the invitation,
All correct!
Please bring decorations, it states
Keep the party secret!
She has brought flowers, a zillion of them;
they would hardly fit in the taxi!
Red, blue, white and mauve,
she wonders who they are for?
But the barn in the middle of nowhere
is empty, no sign of life -
just cows in the meadow chewing the cud....
No mobile reception,
No station, no bus stop....
A long lane home now,
A long shame to bear now,
Heels badly blistered,
Pride sorely wounded,
Rage growling inside her....
Who would play such a mean trick??

SEPTEMBER ON IONA 1

Rose perfume fading
Shadows lengthen, days shorten
Sun tinged by chill breeze

Boats upturned on beach
Tabby cat seeks warmer spot
Ferry brings fewer folk

Flower-scape changes
Atmosphere becomes subdued
Anticipation

SEPTEMBER ON IONA 2

Storm threat on skyline
Rock plants lose their vibrancy
Azure morphs to grey

Sea petrels diving
White-capped waves crashing ashore
Birds and beasts seek shelter

New wisdom dawning,
Captured just for a tide-span
Rest and renewal

A FORGOTTEN BICYCLE

It leans against the old summerhouse,
rusty wheel spokes a nod to its former
glory days as champion of forays into nature.

Wilted bouquets overhang the woven basket:
Withered lilac still murmuring lines from
summer sonnets, sweet pea symphonies with their

spectral arpeggios, rising and falling in cadences,
like gusting leaves across manicured lawns,
chasing away all traces of seasonal depression.

Birds sing full-throated, their daffodil chorus
echoing round the orchard garden,
hedgehogs wake snuffling in the musty woodpile.

At full moon new life throbs through the crippled frame,
sounding the bell in time with the hooting owls,
beckoning fairy folk to mount the saddle, take a ride.

They fly down in the bells of virgin snowdrops,
Filling the basket with crocus and lesser celandine
Speeding to the woods in search of early narcissi.

What stories come to mind as they revel in magical
flight through moonlit meadows and glades.
Released from years of neglect, the old girl lives again

SUMMER COURTYARD

Salvia swaying
by the picket fence, roses
rustling by the gate,
clematis full-bloomed covering
the panes in wild profusion

Bees gently humming
seek honeysuckle's nectar,.
Solstice approaches,
Sweet peas ripple round the pond;
Solace for dark days ahead

DANDELION CLOCKS

Floating on air these frayed threads
of fairy weavers
mark out the cruel
passage of time.

Old men's beards
turned prematurely grey
by life's relentless thrust,
searching for a place
to rest weary heads.

A gentle lightening,
a lifting of melancholy,
the last hurrah as
Old Father Time
calls final orders.

DRAGONFLY

She flew into my cupped hands,
her quivering wings spun from cloud silk,
banishing the inky-black maelstrom
within me, rekindling extinguished
flames of passion, long pulped to ash
in a broken heart.
Together for a nano-second
we tasted eternity.

Section 2

Roses and Thorns:

A Retrospective on Life's

Triumphs & Trials

RESURRECTION OF A SKYLARK

Inspired by Vaughan Williams 'The Lark Ascending'

What if the skylark were reborn,
fledged from within the breast
of a Stradivari violin, attuned to the
heartbeat of wild-flower meadows?

What if the violinist recaptured
that simple bliss in the patchwork of
vetch, clover and oxe-eye daisy,
breathing the petrichor of a post-rain evening?

What if the orchestra returned,
their *musica dolce* releasing fragile
wings in tentative flight, surfing the
rising currents, soaring skywards?

Trilling, trembling, trailing the
cloud-skein of a ripening summer,
honeyed *vibrato* trickling earthwards
in *ritardando*, a gentle enchantment.

If so, then he might live again, fly again,
my lover with wistful green eyes and
hair like spilt sunshine. His soul might
soar where the lark first sang *affetuoso*.

Two hearts might beat in unison again and the
ending become the beginning, grief to joy.
Would we not lie together in that same meadow,
Our love intact, untouchable? *Da capo al fine.*

RASHIDA LAYS AN OFFERING

And when she stoops to lay bouquets of tears,
black apron sorrow spreads wide its broken wings,

her heart leaping in its self-styled prison;
the rhythmic beat of loss pulping thinning bones.

Her daily mudras designed to wash death from
the graceless gravestones, their faded blooms

pearled with putrefaction. She cowers in shadow by
ornate memorials, their pomp disguising power abused,

guilt seeping out into the soil....Nearby a lone thrush
sings a hope-spun solo, lightening the heft of grief.

Angelic hands offer blessings, their empathy soft as
dew-dipped roses, mouthing soundless soliloquies.

Lowering her face into the damp graveside mound
she recalls a man, whose lips were plump with promise,

whose bold words belied his humility, sweet shyness
in the marital bed, a lifetime of selfless love together.

Distant thunderclaps announce avenging gods
descending from an imagined Olympus, bearing

scales of justice, divine intervention on silver salvers...
She silently places her bouquet of tears beneath his tree.

SESTINA FOR A MEDIEVAL BIRTHING

Inspired by a medieval birthing chair in Newark museum

Her chosen godsibbes bring the birthing chair,
She trembles, bravely tries to hide her fear.
Her body now contorted with the pain
she slumps down on the hard seat, grasps the wood.
Sheer terror clouds blue eyes, distorts her face,
as softly her companions start to sing.

But she cares not how sweetly they can sing.
Gripping the hand rails on the oak-hewn chair
she turns to gaze up at her sister's face
and thus encouraged rallies to her fear.
Sparse comfort here from this unyielding wood,
No herbal draft to minimise the pain.

If only they had remedy for her pain!
Yet none to hand; she bravely tries to sing
While cursing in her head the cruel wood
devoid of cushioned pad to sculpt this chair.
As pain levels rise she grapples with her fear
and with her young hands clasps her sweat-stained face.

Through parted fingers now she sees a face,
her husband's, sad to see her writhe in pain.
Dark thoughts of childbirth's dangers bring on fear
his wife may not survive – he cannot sing
with them, pulls up a favourite rocking chair,
distracts himself by carving out of wood

a witch doll from an elm bough in Larks' Wood.
With care he moulds the features of the face
then stands it at the window by his chair,
implores the witch to cast spells for her pain.
He hears the godsibbes as they softly sing
commending her brave efforts, despite fear

her labour is too slow, they start to fear
the baby may be breech. Then from the wood
a magpie calls, drowns out the tune they sing –
Good omen for the mother, so her face
beams radiantly with hope, despite the pain.
With cries and moans she bears down on the chair,

suppressing fear, determined to outface
this brutish wood beneath her. In great pain
she births. They sing and dance around the chair.

A DALLIANCE WITH RACHMANINOFF

Remembering my annus horribilis 1998

October 1998
I'm in prison.
There are no bars, there is no jailer,
I'm marooned here by the deathbed,
Living minute by minute.
His breathing now becoming laboured.
Torment!
Rachmaninoff is playing on the bedroom radio.

November 1998
I'm driving home from hospital,
His death sentence cruelly pronounced.
Such an unforgivable lack of empathy!
In tears I try to imagine being a widow.
Mustn't cry in front of the children though!
Despair
Rachmaninoff is playing on the car radio.

November 12th 1998
I'm standing outside the hospice room,
the one where he died, the one
with blood-red roses outside the window.
I hear my son talking to his father,
Listing all the occasions he'll miss.
Heartbreak!
Rachmaninoff is drifting up from the kitchen.

November 20th 1998
I'm following the coffin,
a single red rose in one hand,
my son's quivering fingers in the other.
This wasn't the plan.
This cold-hearted death betrayed us!
Bereft, alone.
Rachmaninoff is playing on the church organ.

October 2001
Time creeps forward like a snail,
Imperceptibly grief begins to wane.
For three long years my mind has been elsewhere,
But suddenly ... I'm back in my body again!
Feet firmly on the ground.
Triumphant! *I've survived.....*

Maybe it's time to play Rachmaninoff again?

TWO SOULS RETURN IN SEARCH OF A LOST EDEN

In memory of Garry and Judith, forever in my heart

How still it is! Waiting measured in raindrop crotchets,
tapping out time like a metronome:
Calm before storm, day before night.
They drift like clouds, two shifting shapes in the rolling scenery
of a dreary winter stage, frost squeezing the breath
from their lungs, pale figures, poised for a great entrance.

How tense it is; breath exhaled in time with lightning quavers
launched from chthonic clouds,
thunder drumming out a marche funèbre.
Haunting voices whisper warped words, actors delivering
half-swallowed lines, waiting for an off-stage prompt,
arms outstretched like characters in a Shakespearean tragedy.

How great the relief as the spent storm shuffles out to sea,
vacating the stage to a sulphurous sun, suitably tempering
the musical timbre of the setting.
Their presence still palpable, these ghosts emerge from stage left
to play their part again, costumes discarded, true identities exposed,
Adam and Eve, searching in vain for a lost Eden.

GHOST IN AN EMPTY CHAIR

Sometimes it is just a flap of wings in a lonely meadow,
or a child's shoes and socks left by a pond.

Sometimes it is the intensity of darkness
or the emptiness in the kitchen at harvest.

Maybe the laughter ascending from the street below
or the 'stepford wives' promenading past with their pugs,

The elation of cheering crowds at a football match,
the vicar's wife fraternising with the village elite.

Whatever triggers it, you instantly know,
that lonely ghost in the empty chair is you,

as though you are marked out with a blood-red bindi
folk turn away, rejecting the discomfort of your grief.

The world tumbles to wrong conclusions
and your sealed lips shout 'I am still here!'

You cannot fight the inevitability of it;
you ask yourself why grief is such taboo?

Sometimes all it takes is the wind kissing your hair,
the cyclist turning to smile as he pedals past,

moonlight catching the svelte stem of your wine glass,
or an unexpected call from a complete stranger.

Just small things, singular, unremarkable, yet they have
the power to transform your world...and you are grateful.

I AM LISTENING

With homage to Lawrence Ferlinghetti's 'I am waiting'

I ask him if he is listening.
His lips move, they form words,
he nods back......

but his eyes tell a different story....
they are distant, their focus blurred
maybe inventing a fabulous alibi?

I am listening for his apology,
which he is plainly withholding....
pride standing in his way as ever.

And I am listening
for my heart to stop beating,
my distress to find a voice,

for the door bell to chime,
for the children to arrive home,
the baby to howl for its feed,

for the cat crashing through the cat-flap,
live mouse in its jaws
squealing for its mother.

And on a higher level I am listening
for the speeches of politicians
to finally proclaim the whole truth,

for the vicar to preach sermons
with greater relevance to the
truths of a post-modern age,

For the bees to buzz again in gardens
everywhere and the new-born of
endangered species to utter their first cries.

And here and now I am *still* listening for *him*
to explain his ill-judged actions,
to not insult me with bare-faced lies.

But I guess I may be waiting a long time......

FLASHBACK AND PROLEPSIS

Some days we were like birds, flying blind
on winged prayers, in search of Nirvana;

Other days ballerinas, arms draped over the barre,
legs extended in arabesques, practising our pas de deux,

Or wild pheasants with pretensions of grandeur,
craving the pomp of power; shy peacocks

in stolen plumage; Java green embroidered
with iridescent blue, kissing feathers of coppered ochre,

strutting our stuff when the jazz band played - shy girls
with sugar-brown eyes dancing round cheap handbags,

peering coyly from beneath curtain fringes, minds
transported as the dissonant riffs reached a heady climax.

Our world seemed too beautiful, overwhelming,
all sunlit uplands and naked beaches where

summer came but never went. We were there,
clothed in excitement and eager to explore,

quick to respond when chance came calling, soar into
life's blue yonder, outcome unknown, but worth the risk.

Some days now I recall that charming innocence -
Childhood moments of heart-stopping magic; souvenirs

to dine out on in the days of pestilence to follow.
Thankfully we had no inkling then of the darkness to come.

REQUIEM FOR A CELLIST

She rocks rhythmically in her chair,
Her eyes dulled by grief, skeletal fingers
clutching rosary beads. In despair she chants
'Requiem aeternam dona eis, Domine'

The creeping evil nibbles away at her brain,
She clenches her fists, howls
like a caged wolf, searching
desperately for her beloved 'cello.

Then, as if by magic it appears, a Stradivari,
propped up by the Steinway grand,
pleading to be picked up and played again,
its bow sprawled across the piano lid,
resin box still unopened.

A sudden draft from the open window
breathes life back into the stale air.
Haunting sounds unlock iconic images,
transporting her to lovers' beds, concert halls,
summer gardens and back-street alleys -
a heady rush of half-remembered liaisons,
ecstasy and pain intertwined.

Final chords crescendo then trail away
into the invading gloom of a winter twilight.
One last brave 'da capo'- then peace descends.

Her weary frame crumples in dismay,
She attempts to rise from her chair, pleads
one last time: 'Requiem aeternam dona eis, Domine'

MIDNIGHT STARDUST

We come from midnight stardust
And to dust we will finally return.
.
The man in the moon draws a veil across the sky,
Sprinkling the firmament with silver stars.

He creates new wonders with his artist's brush
as we curl up beneath the shimmering counterpane.

Blue affords us the protection of the father,
enfolds us with the nurturing of the mother,

Indigo imbues us with the vision of the third eye
allowing us to see the mystery beyond our frail humanity.

Then when our final night on Earth is spent
And life's dream ebbs away on a Judas tide

We will once more to stardust return.

ANGELA'S PEBBLES

For My Writing Tutor, Angela Locke (Iona retreats 2012- present)

I count her pebbles, hold them silently
to my ear, listening for the familiar voice
buried somewhere within the deep grooves;
alert, waiting for their heaviness to
weigh me down to my knees, dropping
their hushed beauty into the rock pool,
watching them shape-shift beneath the ripples.
I hear the haunting song reverberate
through the shimmering diamonds of gneiss.
Weighing the emptiness in my open hands
I smile. She has returned.

Her spirit travels with the Siren's song,
running with the riptide along the combed beach,
keening with the storm-tossed boats
anchored in the Sound; fanning out across
the yawn of coastal landskein to the hills beyond.
I scry her gentle flight way up above my head,
her sea-green cloak billowing out behind,
ivory petticoats moist with mermaid's sorrow...
I watch the green marble tears tumble to earth,
filling my empty hands with her parting gift.
I weigh their fragility in my closed fists and weep...
She has gone.

A BOX OF PRECIOUS SECRETS

Inside a drawer in grandma's house I find
A secret box with tokens from a tryst
Still wrapped in silk cloth, sealed with rosebud twine.

Victorian postcards, simple, honest, kind,
A silver ring he must have often kissed
Inside a drawer in grandma's house I find.

My heart stands still, it's clear how much he pined
For her, exploring memories of bliss,
Still wrapped in silk cloth sealed with rosebud twine.

A photo of them sitting, arms entwined
Her hair untied in strands of golden mist
Inside a drawer in grandma's house I find

Two hearts in decoupage, both linen-lined
With spidery writing, hard to catch the gist,
Still wrapped in silk cloth, sealed with rosebud twine

I sense that love was always on their mind
And tremble as I touch this precious gift
Inside a drawer in grandma's house I find,
Still wrapped in silk cloth, sealed with rosebud twine.

POSTCARD DREAMS

At the end of the lane you stood still,
photographed wild roses
scented like forgiveness

I thought of the French boudoir,
Peonies spilling from the tipped vase,
Red blood on milk-white sheets.

You laughed that curious bubbling laugh,
Like milk boiling over on the stove,
Afraid to expose your vulnerability.

I remember our time together in Rome,
Chasing barefoot through dusty piazzas,
Dancing to the tune of illicit love.

You bought me an opal ring
from a tramp peddling impossible dreams,
Forgetting that opals bring tears.

Memories are all that survive now,
Blurred, warped by the passing of time,
We cut, paste and save only the best bits.

Our paths ran parallel for a time
but we knew they would never converge -
Postcard dreams, long since consigned to the bin.

SUNDAY MORNING

Memories of growing up by the coast

The gentle hours of morning slip
from the velvet cover of scant moon
over water, stillness so deep it fills
the space like a hypnotic drug.

I rise, heavy-headed and limp-limbed,
flinging wide the casement windows,
gazing down on the shifting shingle of a
single moment, an ever-changing mosaic:

Silhouettes of jet-winged scavengers
pick at mottled sea-scaled pebbles,
triumphantly tugging at skeleton bones
washed up on last night's high tide.

Brine-drenched breakwaters sag beneath
decades of memory, heavy as church lead.
Out to sea sail boats at anchor indulge in the
bliss of a snatched Sunday morning forty winks.

The thinning cloudscape yawns overhead,
casting off the stale sweat of night, as a
chilly off-shore breeze licks at my parched lips.
The town awakes to another sun-drenched Sunday.

IN SEARCH OF THE QUEEN OF DALRIADA*

For Jean, remembering our encounters on Iona

The track is steeped in morning light where
newborn fantasies leap from shadows.
A light breeze lifts the flap of my canvas bag,
where miracles are deftly stored away
from harm, ready for dispersal on the wind -
rescue remedies for doubting pilgrims..

I pause at the Sheila-na-gig, its pagan outlines
carved into ancient stone. My finger mentally
traces the female Yoni high above my head.
Then on into the Christian nunnery, eager to
find more miracles, hidden from prying eyes;
priceless island treasures.

Rounding the corner I see her there, sitting on
the bench in the corner, diamonds in the stone
reflecting Nature's wonder in her eyes, a
paler blue than her school ma'am cardigan
paired daily with the thick tweed skirt.
She turns her face to the weak sun,
finding perfection, delight in just being -
a few precious moments to gain clarity for
her archivist's mind, now muddled by life.

I remember the face in the flagstones I saw
when we were first together in the Abbey.
She never forgot that, thought it was maybe
Jesus, although there was much more she did forget,
that last year she came. That was her swan song,
at peace, wrapped in a cloak of island comfort..

I join her there on the bench, bathed in the glint
of lewisian gneiss, with the chanting of the nuns,
the midnight bubbles still blowing round her head.
Releasing the catch on my bag I open it wide
and watch the miracles fly into her lap.
She is forever Queen of Dalriada– I am just
another pilgrim seeking to bottle the elixir of truth..

---

* **Dalriada**, *Irish Dál Riada or Riata, Gaelic kingdom that, at least from the 5th century AD, extended on both sides of the North Channel and composed the northern part of the present County Antrim, Northern Ireland, and part of the Inner Hebrides.*

SONNET FOR THREE SACRED OBJECTS

I linger here, hoping I may invoke
Healing from angels clothed in chakra cloaks,
As reverently they stand knee deep in prayer
Like holy monks in robes with tonsured hair.
Close by a goddess sits and waits alone,
A Maltese lady, carved from ancient stone.
Her face is blank, no mouth, no ears, no eye,
A replica they say from times gone by.
Alongside stands a wise and cherished Tree
Of Eden, juicy apples dangling free.
A Wise Man's star on top, a fitting crown,
It feels like Paradise is smiling down.
So patiently these precious objects wait
To open up for me the sacred gate.

THE POET AT NIGHT

A Celebration of the Joy of Writing Poetry

Solitude,
the breathing in of pure peace;
the world outside in silent indifference.

Virtual sonnets
ripe for inscription dance across
the linen canvas of a blotting paper sky.

An overwhelming freedom
unleashes limitless fantasies
streamed from the super-charged brain.

Night is the zenith
of poetic endeavour,
sacrosanct, the Muse fully invested.

Moonlight filters through
a chink in the shutters,
releasing the wisdom of Selene,

lunar goddess. She descends
in her chariot of winged horses,
blessing the poet with imagistic words..

Dawn brings finality;
a triumph of poetic expression.
Deep sleep is ample reward.

ACKNOWLEDGEMENTS:

The following poems first appeared in the magazines as listed below

The Blue Nib Literary Magazine
Ghost in an Empty Chair
Postcard Dreams
Sunday Morning
Flashback and Prolepsis
Lady with Lavender Aura

Impspired Magazine
A Dementia Sufferer attempts Rewilding
I am Listening
Requiem for a Cellist
In search of the Queen of Dalriada
Sonnet For Three Sacred Objects
A Box of Precious Secrets

Hedgehog Poetry Press Anthology
The Holly and The Ivy

My sincere thanks to my friend Marian Williamson for use of her artwork to illustrate the postcard bookmarks.
© Marian Williamson 'We tasted Eternity' (illustrating my 'Dragonfly' poem)